The Trump Presidensy

#1 best selling book "EVER"

by R.L. Corbo

DORRANCE
PUBLISHING CO
EST. 1920
PITTSBURGH, PENNSYLVANIA 15238

Dorrance Publishing Co
585 Alpha Drive
Pittsburgh, PA 15238
Visit our website at *www.dorrancebookstore.com*

ISBN: 978-1-4809-9354-9
eISBN: 978-1-4809-9361-7

Welcome to the world of President Donald Trump. Donalds first year was a doozy. As any Stand up Comedian, or Cartoonist will tell you, its way too much material coming in way too fast. Its a Trump overload. Heres a small sample of whats gone on in the first year of the Trump Presidensy.

So take this book into the bathroom, have a seat and enjoy. Remember all this stuff is real, it just might make you puke.

Enjoy

(1)

March
of
the
Executive's

Principal Dan

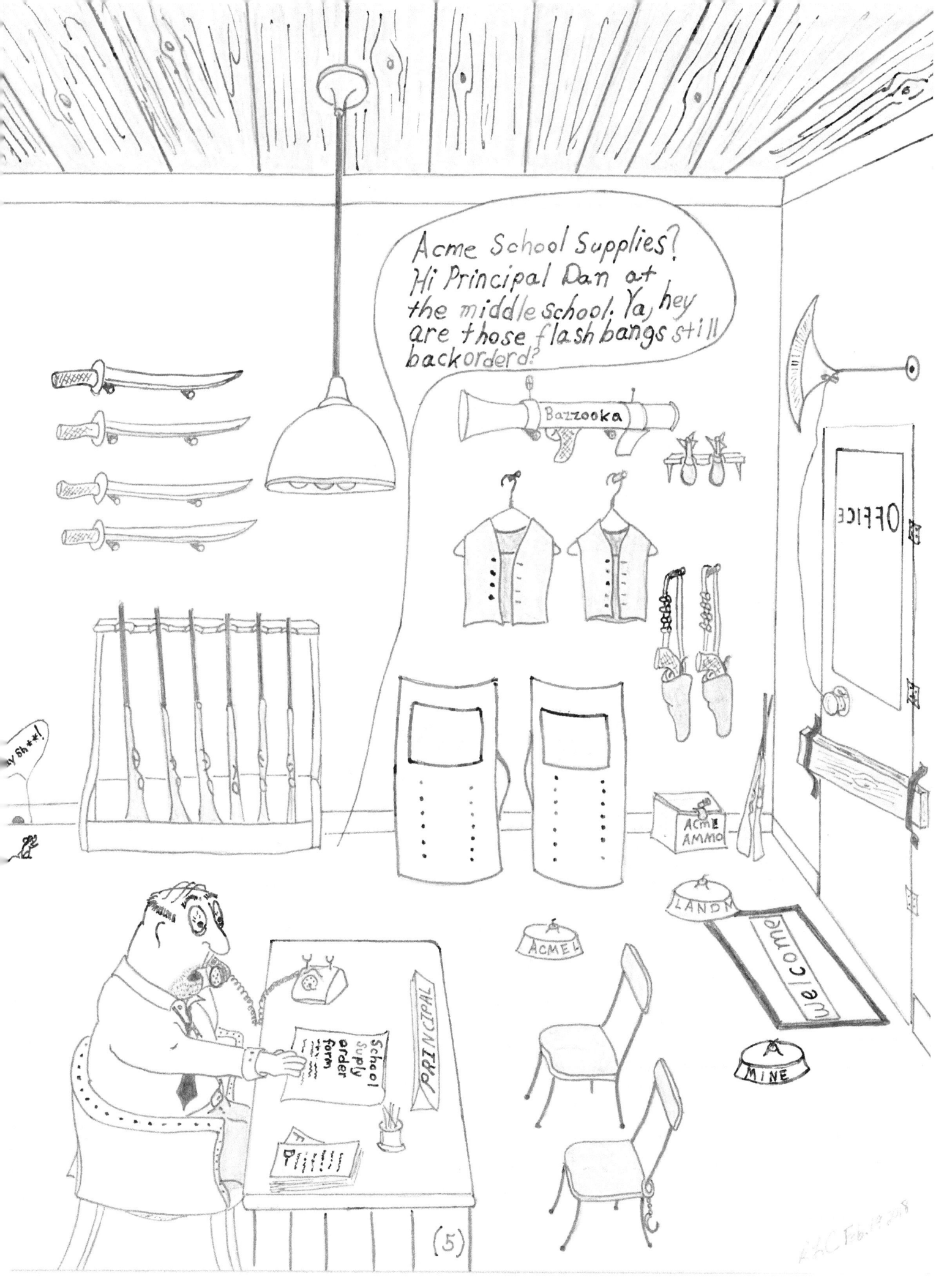

Who's The Prisoner Here ?

Who's advising the Donald now that Steve is gone?

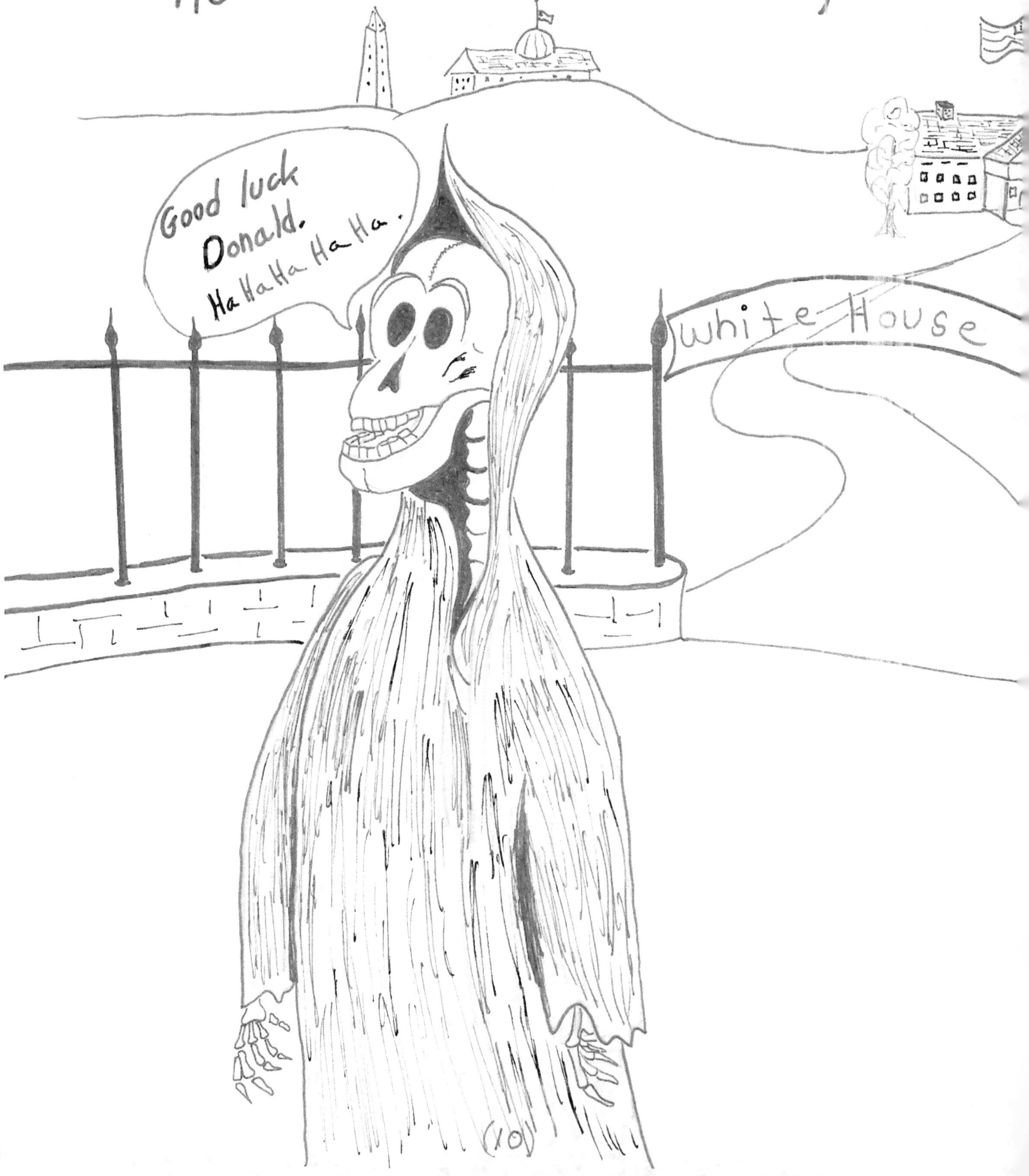

Trumps War

Trumps Grand Parade

"It was Huge"

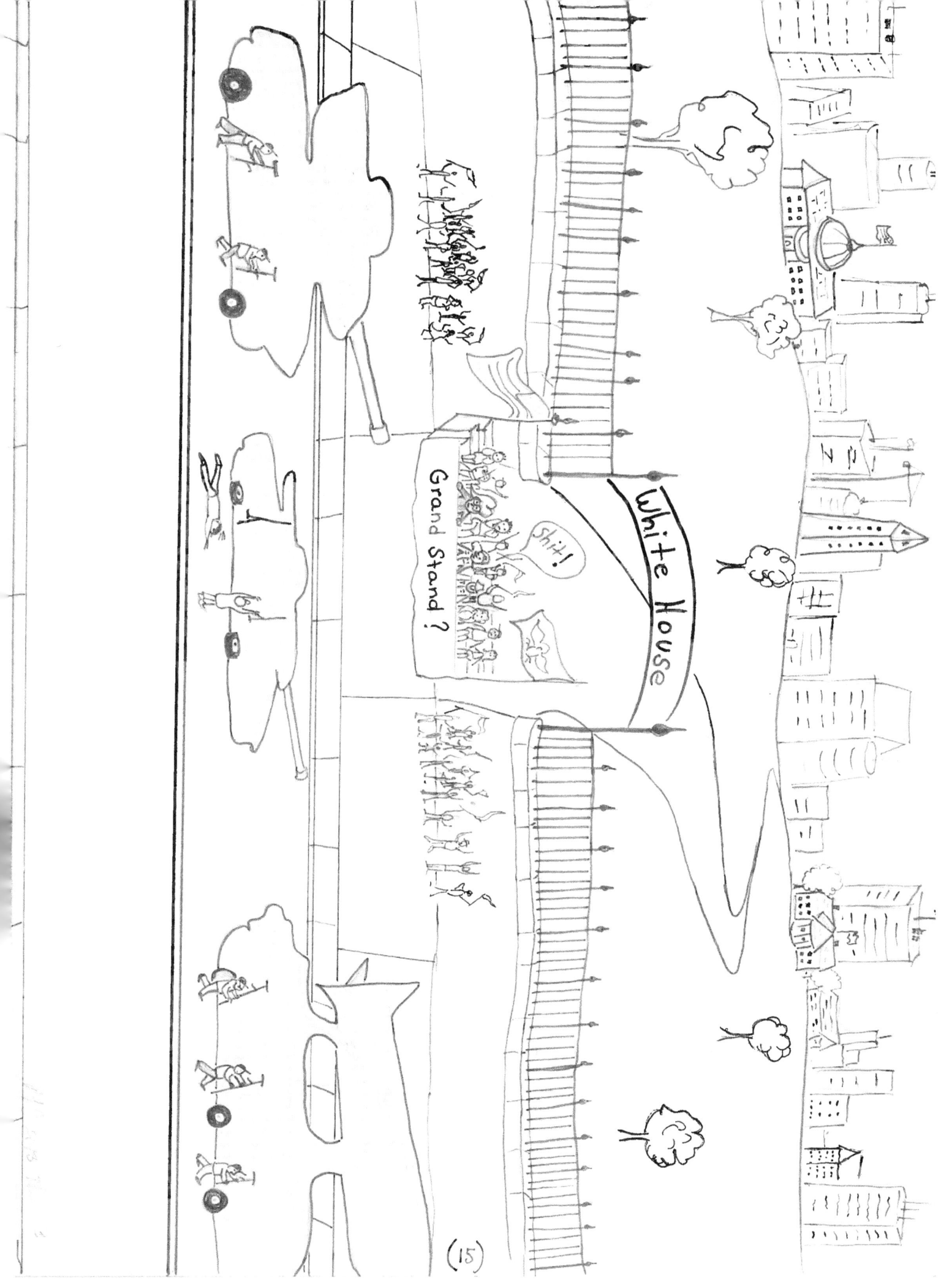

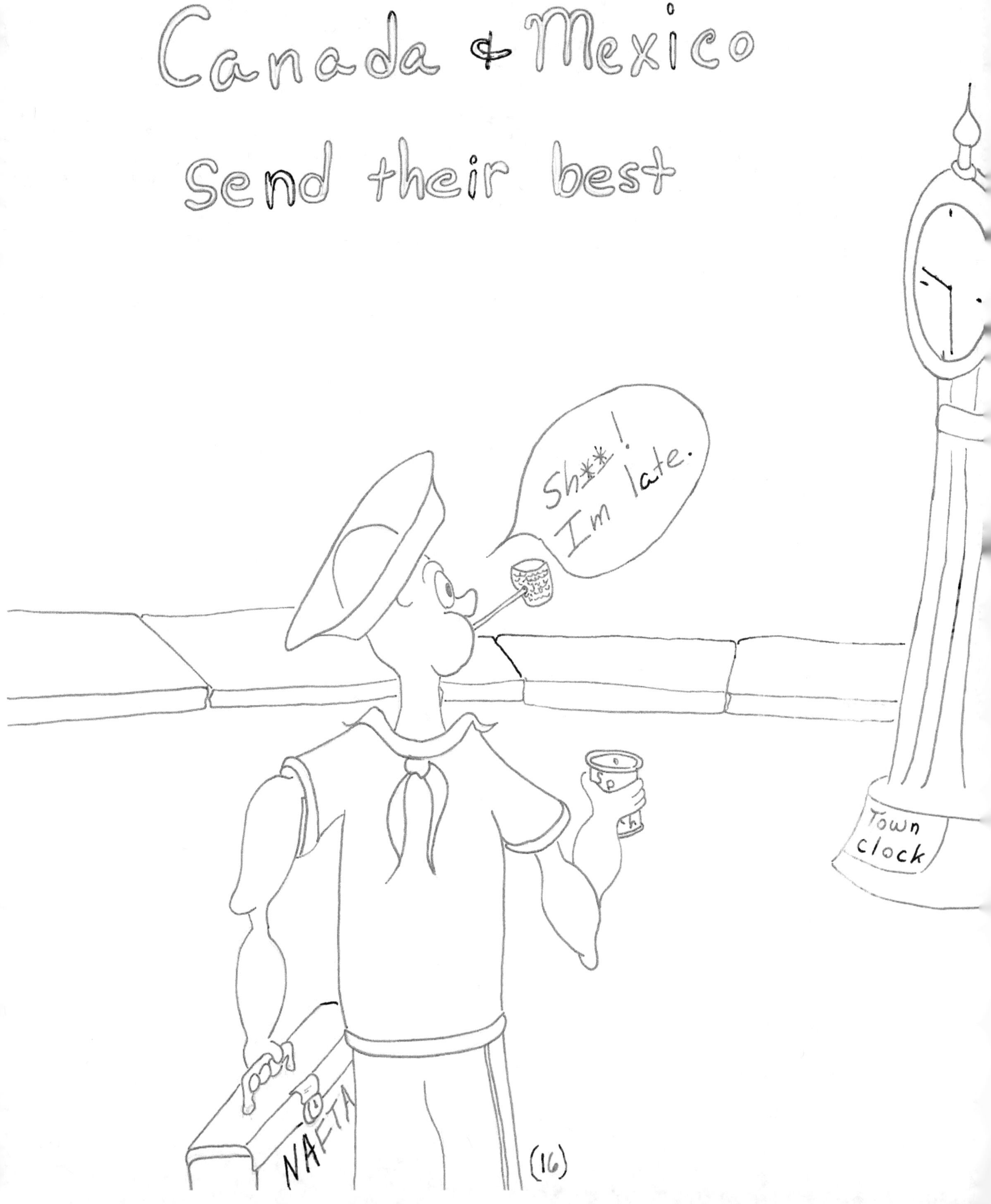
Canada & Mexico
send their best
Sh**! Im late.
Town clock
NAFTA

The Best Wall "EVER"

we love Emperor Ming

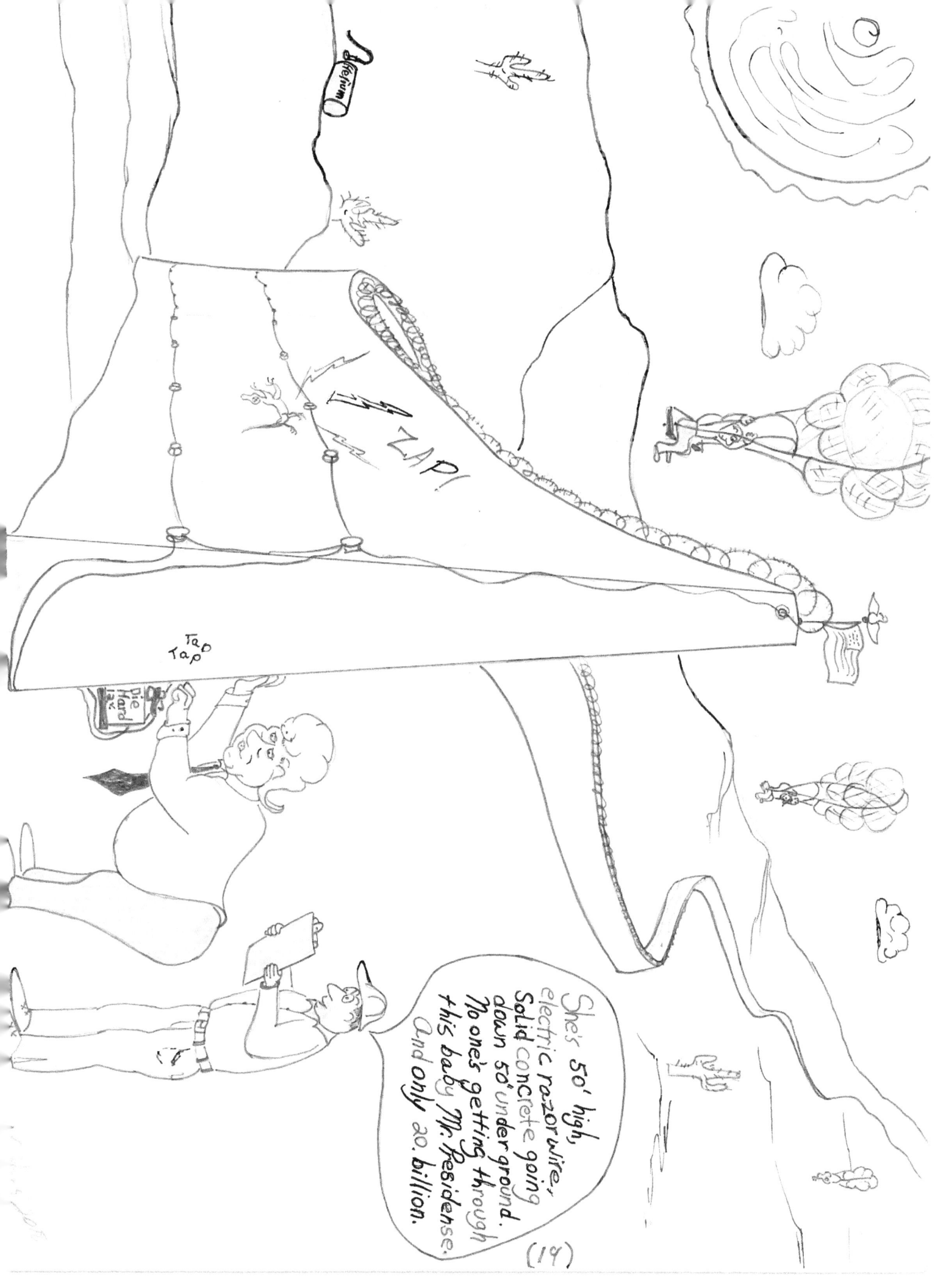

At least he stirred things up a little.

Have You Seen Donald?

(23)

Whats really going on?

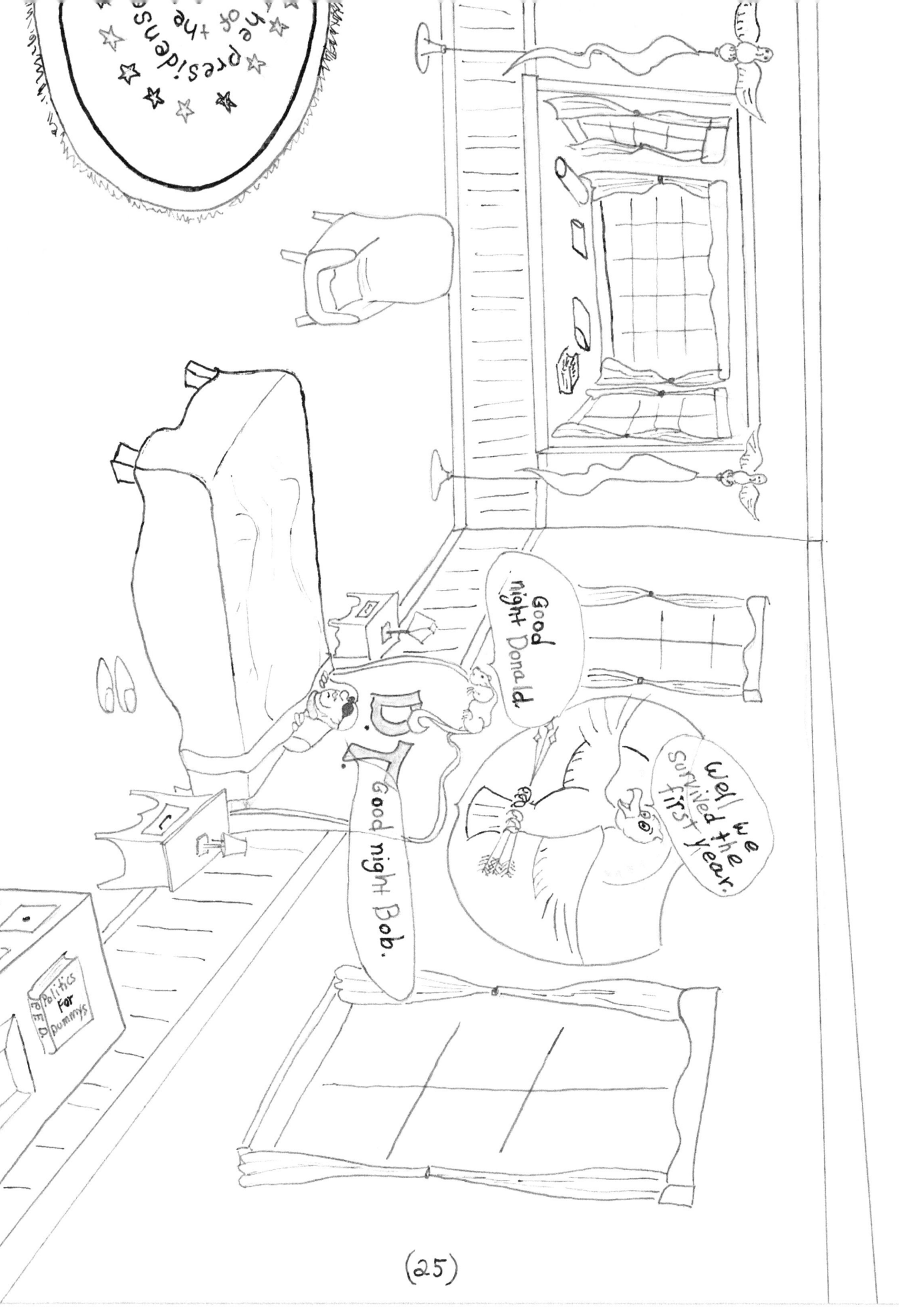

Well thats the first year.
If were lucky Donald will
make it through year #2.
Volume 2 is under way.

Lets hope we make it,
things could get a little
Stormy.

The Summit

THE
END

REALLY?